# Religion as Reinforcement in Hemingway

BY

James I. McGovern

WingSpan Press

Copyright © 2013 by James I. McGovern

All rights reserved.

No part of this book may be reproduced or transmitted in any form or by any means, electronic or mechanical, including photocopying, recording or by any information storage and retrieval system, without written permission from the author, except for the inclusion of brief quotations in review.

Published in the United States and the United Kingdom by WingSpan Press, Livermore, CA

The WingSpan name, logo and colophon are the trademarks of WingSpan Publishing.

ISBN 978-1-59594-504-4

First edition 2013

Printed in the United States of America

www.wingspanpress.com

Library of Congress Control Number: 2013948531

1 2 3 4 5 6 7 8 9 10

# Contents

1. Technically Religious ............................................. 1

2. The Clergy and Prayer ............................................ 9

3. Christian Tradition and Church Power ................. 25

4. Non-Religious Beliefs and Values ....................... 45

5. Believing in Belief ................................................ 61

    Bibliography .......................................................... 69

    About the Author .................................................. 73

# 1. Technically Religious

Born in 1899 of Protestant parents, Ernest Hemingway was baptized a Catholic in 1918 during his military service in Italy. He soon discontinued his practice of Catholicism, but returned to it once more in 1926, largely to facilitate his marriage to Pauline Pfeiffer. This attention to religion is also apparent in Hemingway's frequent treatment of religious material in his works. This treatment, and the influences that determined it, comprise the subject of the present study.

Religion, as it will be discussed in this study, includes both the codified and the implied beliefs of Christianity, and the formalized methods of their expression. The pagan and Judaic origins of Christian belief are, of course, essential to their meaning, so that these non-Christian aspects of religion are implicit in its definition. The formalized expression of the beliefs, it should be understood, includes those forms and institutions, such as the hierarchies within religious bodies, which have such expression as their function.

Given this definition, one becomes aware that, despite the presence of a large amount of religious material in Hemingway's works, religion itself does not provide the themes of his works. One is struck, instead, by the reinforcing nature of religious material upon the major thematic thrusts. This suggests the thesis that is to be tested in this study: that Hemingway treated religion as a thing of secondary importance, a social phenomenon of value to the extent that it reinforces beliefs that one already holds. This is not to deny the possibility of religion functioning on a personal basis for a character, for his beliefs and ways of expressing them might serve to reveal the writer's primary theme, thereby reinforcing the *writer's* ideas.

In discussing this thesis, it will be helpful to begin by relating some more detailed biographical information regarding Hemingway's religious background and development. The remainder of this chapter, therefore, will be devoted to this end, as well as to noting some strong correlations between the man's experience and incidents in his works. In this way, it can be established that Hemingway's treatment of religion in his works does reflect, to a degree, his own religious background and development. Unless otherwise noted, the factual information here is derived from Baker's comprehensive biography (Carlos Baker, *Ernest Hemingway: A Life Story* (New York, 1969)).

When Hemingway was christened at Oak Park's First Congregational Church, both his given names were from his mother's side of the family–Ernest for his grandfather, and Miller for his great-uncle. This fact is indicative of his mother's influence in household affairs, a factor that was to contribute greatly to Hemingway's alienation from his Protestant background. His father was outwardly strong and assertive, but it was Ernest's mother who usually prevailed in disagreements. His father was quite strict, insisting on full observance of the Lord's Day and punishing misbehavior with a razor strop, the punishment followed by injunctions to kneel and ask God's forgiveness. But such values could only impress Ernest by their ineffectiveness, their holder so often yielding before his wife, who spanked with a hairbrush, not a razor strop, and observed the Lord's Day by singing in the choir loft.

Julanne Isabelle concludes that his father's lack of conviction was probably most influential on young Hemingway when it was concerned with moral issues. (Julanne Isabelle, *Hemingway's Religious Experience* (New York, 1964), p. 19.) This self-doubt can be seen in "The Doctor and the Doctor's Wife," an early short story. The doctor's wife causes her husband to doubt his conviction that Dick Boulton was evading payment of a bill by creating a row. She supports her argument by quoting the Bible. The doctor stalks off teeming with frustration, even though his wife is neither forceful nor convincing. The frustration stems from his own inner doubts, which suggests that the principles by which he lives are insufficient.

That the doctor in this story is based on Hemingway's father, who also was a doctor, can be safely inferred; the name of Dick Boulton is too similar to that of Nick Boulton, a half-breed sawyer who worked for a lumbering outfit near Dr. Hemingway's woodland property, to be a coincidence. This same lack of conviction, then, was seen by young Hemingway in his father, and it greatly helped to alienate the growing boy from his Protestant heritage. This is not to dismiss the possible influence of his mother's religion; if it was as brutal and arid as expressed in the story, it was probably significant in young Hemingway's alienation.

The alienation from Protestantism apparently

predisposed Hemingway to conversion, for he became a Catholic while serving in World War I. In a letter written in 1945, he explained his action in this way: "In 1918, said he, he had been very frightened after his wounding, and therefore very devout. He feared death, believed in personal salvation, and thought that prayer to the Virgin and various saints might produce results." (Baker, p. 449.) Baker's summary of this letter will be quoted again later, in reference to another point.

Another probable influence on his conversion was a young priest named Don Giuseppi Bianchi, who came from the Abruzzi. Father Bianchi was a chaplain in the Brigata Ancona, with which Hemingway was stationed. They would meet in the officers' mess and the priest quickly befriended Hemingway, who treated him with sympathy and respect. After he was wounded, Hemingway was anointed by this priest. Father Bianchi, it seems, was the prototype for the priest in *A Farewell to Arms*, for the latter priest also came from the Abruzzi, met with Frederick Henry in the officers' mess, and visited Henry after he was wounded.

Hemingway's conversion proved to be short-lived, for he ceased to practice Catholicism shortly after his return to America. When he wished to marry Pauline Pfeiffer, however, it was necessary for him to again become a practicing Catholic. Although his return to Catholicism was primarily for practical reasons, Hemingway later claimed to have made a serious effort to incorporate the practice of Catholicism into his way of life. In a letter written in 1927, he explained his position: "For many years, wrote Ernest, he had been a Catholic, although he had fallen away badly in the period 1919-

27, during which time he did not attend communion. But he had gone regularly to Mass, he said, during 1926 and 1927, and had definitely set his house in order (his phrase) in 1927." (Baker, p. 185.) It should be noted, however, that his explanation was made in reply to a Dominican priest's inquiry, and was made, according to Baker, "rather lamely."

This conception of his own status as a Catholic, from 1919-27, is mirrored in Hemingway's characterization of Jake Barnes, the narrator of *The Sun Also Rises*. Jake succinctly expresses his position in an exchange with Bill Gorton:

> "Listen, Jake," he said, "are you really a Catholic?"
> "Technically."
> "What does that mean?"
> "I don't know."

Jake later attends Mass and, rather lamely, tells Brett Ashley that he is religious. His position, however, appears to be similar to that of Hemingway in 1926, the year of the novel's publication. Like his creator, Jake tries to incorporate the practice of Catholicism into his way of life, but he cannot seem to identify with the values themselves. For both, Catholicism seems to be something forced on one's self, rather than an actual belief.

Hemingway's inability to accept Pauline's religion contributed to the failure of their marriage, but his non-acceptance is, in turn, attributable largely to another influence, his experience in the Spanish Civil War. "The only way he could run his life decently was to accept

## Religion as Reinforcement in Hemingway

the discipline of the Church. But the problem in Spain was that the Church had sided with the enemy. This fact bothered him so much that he had even quit praying: it seemed somehow 'crooked' to have anything to do with a religious institution so closely allied to Fascism." (Baker, p. 333.) This political situation in Spain, and the Church's role in it, are described extensively in *For Whom the Bell Tolls*, published in 1940, the year of Hemingway's divorce from Pauline. That he had quit praying is not surprising, given the impressions rendered in this novel, and the treatment of prayer itself is particularly effective. The latter point will be discussed in detail in the next chapter.

Following his divorce from Pauline, Hemingway never again practiced a formal religion. In the letter of 1945 referred to earlier, Hemingway revealed that "Deprived of the ghostly comforts of the Church, yet unable to accept as gospel the secular substitutes which Marxism offered, he had abandoned his simplistic faith in the benefits of personal petition and turned, like his hero Robert Jordan, to embrace a doctrine of 'life, liberty, and the pursuit of happiness.'" (Baker, p. 449.) Hemingway continued, however, to use much religious material in his works, and never became really anti-religious. Late in 1958, in fact, when his friend Gary Cooper told Hemingway that he'd yielded to his wife's persuasion and become a Catholic, Hemingway was sympathetic. He told the actor that he had done the same thing thirty years before, and that he still "believed in belief." (Baker, p. 543.)

Hemingway's use of the indefinite term "belief" is significant for the purposes of this study. It indicates the mature writer's esteem for an organized set of values by which to live, but its generality discredits the notion that he was endorsing some particular set of doctrines. In the chapters that follow, which will examine Hemingway's treatment of religion in his works, the primary stress will be on the relationship between aspects of religion and the individual values evinced by Hemingway or instilled in his characters. It will be determined whether Hemingway did indeed treat religion as a thing of secondary importance, a social phenomenon of value to the extent that it reinforces beliefs that one already holds. Due consideration will also be given to its possible function on personal bases for individual characters, and the consequent reinforcement of Hemingway's own beliefs.

## 2. The Clergy and Prayer

This chapter, and the next one, will concern Hemingway's treatment of several aspects of Christianity in his works. This chapter will deal with his treatment of the clergy and of prayer. The next chapter will deal with his treatment of traditional beliefs and practices, and of (Catholic) Church authority.

An early treatment of the clergy occurs in "The Gambler, the Nun, and the Radio." This story is based, according to Baker, on Hemingway's experience in a Billings, Montana, hospital, where he was confined for treatment of a broken arm. The hospital, St. Vincent's, was run by the Sisters of Charity of Leavenworth, and one of them, Sister Florence, became Hemingway's favorite visitor. Baker describes her as "a gentle nun who loved baseball and believed strongly that the Lord could be persuaded to intercede in human affairs. Her prayers had been answered during the World Series of October. Ernest loved to see her and to hear her breathless talk." (Baker, p. 218.)

Sister Florence became Sister Cecilia in the short story. Sister Cecilia's gentleness is manifested in her concern for Cayetano, the small-time gambler, and her love of sports in her anxiety over a Notre Dame football game. Her confidence in the Lord's intercession is manifested in her prayers for Cayetano's recovery and a Notre Dame victory. The story's protagonist, Mr.

## Religion as Reinforcement in Hemingway

Frazer, enjoys her company at his bedside, as well as her conversation, which is the "breathless talk" of Sister Florence.

The most impressive traits of Sister Cecilia, however, are revealed rather late in the story. "When I was a girl," she tells Frazer, "I thought if I renounced the world and went into the convent I would be a saint. That was what I wanted to be and that was what I thought I had to do to be one. . . . All I want is to be a saint. That is all I've ever wanted." Frazer approves of her ambition and encourages her to persist in the way of life she's adopted. In doing so, however, he does not express acceptance of this way of life for himself or endorse the religion she has drawn on to order her life and the values by which she lives it. Frazer's liking for the nun is due to her personal traits, not her religion, but it is only logical that he should encourage her to live in a way that will preserve those traits he admires.

Religion is no more of a factor in Hemingway's positive treatment of Sister Cecilia than in Frazer's liking for her. The nun is presented positively because she is gentle and comforting and, more significantly, because she has definite values by which to order her life. Her Catholicism is of value for the order she derives from it, as Frazer orders his sleepless nights by the radio broadcasts. Hemingway's evaluation of Sister Cecilia, then, is made on the basis of her personal traits and values, not the religion which encourages those traits and orders those values. An important implication of viewing religion in this way is that religion is a thing of practical value to a man during his natural lifetime, rather than a set of instructions for attaining supernatural bliss. It further implies that an individual, such as Sister Cecilia, for whom religion functions in this practical way, is an admirable person.

A more extensive treatment of the clergy occurs in *A Farewell to Arms*. The priest who befriends Frederick Henry, as related in the previous chapter, is based on the priest who anointed Hemingway a Catholic in 1918. Frederick Henry not only admires the priest as an individual but actually identifies with his values. Thus, the treatment of this member of the clergy goes a step beyond the treatment of Sister Cecilia. The priest, in turn, serves a more significant function in the rendering of Hemingway's theme.

This function first becomes apparent when the priest invites Henry to visit his home town of Capracotta in the Abruzzi. The priest's description of his town is quite appealing to Henry, who sees in it a locale entirely opposite to that in which he is then situated. As the novel progresses, and Henry becomes increasingly alienated from the war and the negative values associated with it, he is increasingly attracted to the priest's home and the values expressed and manifested by the priest. An article by Baker delineates the opposing concepts in Henry's consciousness:

> Each is a kind of poetic intuition, charged with emotional values and woven, like a cable, of many strands. The Home-concept, for example, is associated with the mountains; with dry, cold weather; with peace and quiet; with love, dignity, health, happiness, and the good life; and with worship, or at least the consciousness of God. The

> Not-home concept is associated with with low-lying plains; with rain and fog; with obscenity, indignity, suffering, nervousness, war, and death; and of course with irreligion. (Carlos Baker, "The Mountain and the Plain," Virginia Quarterly Review, 27 (1951), 413.)

The Abruzzi homeland of the priest is high in the mountains; it is described as cold, clear, dry country. It eventually becomes the goal not only of Henry, but of Catherine Barkley as well. Together, they flee from the war to a satisfying way of life on the mountainside above Montreux. This, as Baker points out in the article cited above, is "the closest approach to the priest's fair homeland in the Abruzzi that they are ever to know." (P. 415.) Henry's attainment of genuine, albeit temporary, fulfillment evinces the priest's significance in the novel. It is the priest's values, and the locale which Henry associates with them, that Henry strives toward and partially attains in his short-lived happiness with Catherine.

The actual values of the priest, for the purposes of this study, are not actually as important as their relationship to his religion. In this vein, it should be noted that Henry, although he is increasingly attracted to the priest's personal values, never seriously considers adopting the priest's religion. Hemingway himself, of course, was anointed a Catholic by the prototype of the priest in *A Farewell to Arms*, but the novel was written after Hemingway had ceased to practice. Henry likes the priest for his personal traits, as Mr. Frazer liked Sister Cecilia, and Henry goes further by identifying with the priest's personal values. But Hemingway does not have his protagonist adopt the priest's formal religious beliefs; they are not included among the values that motivate Henry toward the novel's climax. The priest's religion, in fact, is not at the core of his own values; rather, it conveniently embodies his personal virtues and orders his personal values. This is seen in his advice to Henry that he should love God:

> "You should love him."
> "I don't love much."
> "Yes," he said, "You do. What you tell me about in the nights. That is not love. That is only passion and lust. When you love you wish to do things for. You wish to sacrifice for. You wish to serve."
> "I don't love."
> "You will. I know you will. Then you will be happy."

Thus, the priest's charity and his esteem for self-sacrifice are conveniently embodied by his religion. The virtues and values he manifests have their roots in his personality, however, not in the formal religion he practices.

Hemingway's positive treatment of the priest is due partially to the priest's kindness and quiet courage, and to his personal values, which are antithetical to the to the absurdity and misery of war. Most significant, however, is that the priest's values are definite and ordered, so that he has a definite code by which to live. His Catholicism provides this order, and in this way functions as reinforcement. It could, conceivably, function in this way for Henry if he were able, as Hemingway was in 1918, to accept the technical beliefs and practices of Catholicism. Henry, however, seems only slightly more interested in Catholicism than Mr. Frazer, so that religion is not likely to work for him as it does for the priest. Hemingway's evaluation of the priest, then, is made on the basis of his virtues and personal values, not the religion which embodies those virtues and orders those values.

The membership of Sister Cecilia and the priest in religious orders provided them a constant means of practicing their religion. For Hemingway's religious lay characters, however, the most readily available means is prayer. His treatment of this practice in his works will comprise the remainder of this chapter. The prayers referred to will be categorized according to the characters' motives and the circumstances in which the prayers are expressed. The basic function of prayer in Hemingway's works can then be deduced from the similarities in the functions of the various types.

One type of prayer depicted by Hemingway is that which stems from selfish motives and is, by this basic characteristic, best distinguished. In *The Sun Also Rises*, for example, Brett complains to Jake that praying "Never does me any good. I've never gotten anything I prayed for." Brett's conception of prayer as a means of getting things may be due to naivete, the lack of instruction in a formal religion. Yet Jake, who attempts to practice his professed Catholicism, also does not know how to pray. This is reflected in his visit to the cathedral shortly after his arrival in Pamplona:

I knelt and started to pray and prayed for everybody I thought of, Brett and Mike and Bill and Robert Cohn and myself, and all the bull-fighters, separately for the ones I liked, and lumping all the rest, then I prayed for myself again, and while I was praying for myself I found I was getting sleepy, so I prayed that the bull-fights would be good, and that it would be a fine fiesta, and that we would get some fishing. I wondered if there was anything else I might pray for, and I thought I would like to have some money, so I prayed that I would make a lot of money . . .

There is some selfishness in Jake's praying, since he prays more for the bullfighters he personally likes, and since he prays to obtain material benefits such as entertaining bullfights, good fishing, and money. However, the monotonous rhythm of the passage, as well as its lack of direction, suggests that the praying itself is a comforting experience for Jake. The strange atmosphere of the cathedral provides a sanctuary from the thoughts of Brett's and his own sexual problems; the latter thoughts are replaced by his rambling internal prayer. In this way, prayer seems to function on a personal basis for Jake, who feels guilty as a result. Later in the passage, he senses an incongruence between his praying and what prayer should be, stating that "I was a little ashamed, and regretted that I was such a rotten Catholic."

In *For Whom the Bell Tolls*, Hemingway's novel of

the Spanish Civil War, there are instances of prayer for one cause directed against prayer for the opposing cause. These prayers, to the same God on behalf of opposing interests, create irony. An example of this irony occurs shortly after the extermination of El Sordo's band by Lt. Berrendo. As the Fascist officer rides with his men past the hidden Anselmo, he prays for a comrade killed in the recent battle. That he should invoke the Blessed Virgin with El Sordo's poncho-wrapped head flapping against his horse's flanks is ironic in itself. A greater irony, however, is seen in Anselmo's praying the same prayer for Berrendo's victims as he returns to camp, going on to ask the Lord to help him fight well against Berrendo the following day. The prayer by each man for his own cause is an extension of the selfish prayer discussed above. The context in which the prayers appear produces an ironic effect emphasizing the desire of each for temporal advantage. The prayers might also be interpreted as attempts to impose order, to rationalize or obtain sanction for the acts of war. The irony remains, however, for the basis of rationalization or agent of sanction is the same for both sides.

That Anselmo and other Loyalists in the novel should pray is, of course, contradictory to their professed atheism. The contradiction seems best explained by the fact that the Loyalists, like the enemy, had been taught to accept Catholicism from their earliest years. For one to truly forsake a belief held for so long is very difficult, and one will probably regress to that belief when his faith in the new cause is shaken. This phenomenon is manifested by young Joaquin, whose death takes place amidst another scene of ironic prayer.

James I. McGovern

The actual extermination of El Sordo's band presents ironic prayers in a more intense setting. Young Joaquin, as the small group is about to be wiped out, fervently recites the Hail Mary and the Act of Contrition. As he fervently repeats the closing words of the Act of Contrition over and over again, a bomb hits and knocks him unconscious. He is then approached by Berrendo who, with a single brief gesture, renders the boy's prayers ironic:

> Joaquin was bleeding from the nose and from the ears. He had known nothing and had no feeling since he had suddenly been in the very heart of the thunder and the breath had been wrenched from his body when the one bomb struck so close and Lieutenant Berrendo made the sign of the cross and then shot him in the back of the head, as quickly and as gently, if such an abrupt movement can be gentle, as Sordo had shot the wounded horse.

As he walks down the hill, Berrendo recites five Our Fathers and five Hail Marys for the dead comrade he later prays for while passing Anselmo. Unlike Anselmo's petition to perform well, Joaquin's prayers were simply for survival. Nevertheless, they become ironic when Berrendo, invoking the same deity, proves the boy's prayers futile. Futility, in fact, seems more characteristic of the prayers in these passages than desire for temporal advantage. The natural consequence of Berrendo shooting Joaquin in the head, after all, is not in the least affected by the boy's prayers or the lieutenant's sign of the cross, and Berrendo's comrade is just as dead for the officer's prayers as he would be otherwise.

The prayers of Anselmo referred to above are, we are told in the novel, his first since the start of the revolution. Earlier in the novel, it is revealed that, in times past, the saying of prayers functioned for Anselmo by relieving his loneliness. During the revolution, "He missed the prayers but he thought it would be unfair and hypocritical to say them and he did not wish to ask any favors or for any different treatment than all the men were receiving." Thus, by opposing the side which the Church supported, Anselmo, like Hemingway, was "deprived of the ghostly comforts of the Church." (Baker, p. 449.) However, whereas prayer functioned for Anselmo on a very personal basis by relieving his loneliness, his religion itself functioned in quite a different way.

The function of religion for Anselmo is revealed during his long watch on the mountainside. In the Catholic faith Anselmo sees a means of atonement for such great sins as the killing he must do in the war. "If we no longer have religion after the war," he considers, "then I think there must be some form of civic penance organized that all may be cleansed from the killing or else we will never have a true and human basis for living." Anselmo's regret for losing his religion, then, is due to his no longer having the Church available as a means to discharge his guilt. Although prayer is likely a part of Anselmo's conception of penance, the passage just quoted shows that it's the institution, rather than the practice, that he conceives as supplying atonement. In this way, religion, as opposed to prayer, functions on a less personal yet more significant basis for the character Anselmo.

An important implication of Anselmo's need for a social institution to discharge his guilt is that the individual, by his own efforts, is unable to rectify the harm resulting from his misdeeds. It takes a greater authority than oneself to grant atonement, an authority that is formal and recognized; private prayers for forgiveness do not bring a formal response, and are therefore insufficient. What Anselmo is seeking is a secular equivalent of the Catholic Church, an institution that will provide principles by which he can be sure to live decently, to "have a true and human basis for living." By establishing these principles, which he is unable to establish for himself, the institution will serve to order his way of life, a function once served for him by the Church.

Although prayer functions for Anselmo on a very personal basis, his prayers do not manifest the intense desire for temporal advantage found in the prayers of other Hemingway characters. At times, the intensity is so great that the praying is done in desperation. An example of desperate prayer is found in the seventh vignette of *In Our Time*, which depicts a soldier, in the midst of a bombardment, praying to Christ that he might survive. Although his prayers are apparently answered, he does not, as he promised in his desperation, tell everyone in the world that Christ is the only thing that matters. Instead, he goes to a brothel the next night and never tells anyone about Christ. The soldier's prayer was motivated by his urge for self-preservation; it was his only recourse in the circumstance of his helplessness. The latter circumstance made his prayer desperate, and his desperation employed insincerity. A desperate prayer seems to be a selfish prayer in its purest form, and the insincerity seen in this example is probably, therefore, latent in the examples cited earlier, the other instances of praying to get things.

Another example of desperate prayer is seen in *A Farewell to Arms*. It occurs late in the novel, when Henry desperately prays that Catherine survive her Caesarean:

> Oh, God, please don't let her die. I'll do anything for you if you won't let her die. Please, please, please, dear God, don't let her die. Dear God, don't let her die. Please, please, please, don't let her die. God please make her not die. I'll do anything you say if you don't let her die. You took the baby but don't let her die. That was all right but don't let her die. Please, please, dear God, don't let her die.

Henry's prayer is desperate for largely the same reasons as the appeal of the soldier of *In Our Time*. Although not praying for his own life, like the soldier, Henry's appeal is for a life which hangs in the balance, namely, the life of Catherine. Like the soldier, Henry is helpless to do anything but pray. The latter circumstance causes his prayer to be desperate, and his desperation employs insincerity, as Henry promises, like the soldier, to "do anything" if his prayer is answered. Henry's prayer, therefore, is another prayer purely to get something, and its desperate expression more clearly shows the motive from which it stems.

From a psychological standpoint, it seems that Henry and the other characters are trying, with their prayers, to resolve their immediate conflicts and, thereby, adjust to their immediate situations. Unable to find solutions to their problems that they themselves can accomplish, they externalize the agent of solution. The appeal to this agent is prayer, and by praying they are doing all they can to solve their problems, thereby resolving the conflict between the realization of their problems and the realization of their helplessness. Thus, prayer offers a degree of relief from conflicts, and yields these characters an adjustment of sorts.

In addition to stemming from the desire for temporal advantage, prayers spoken in Hemingway's works sometimes are insincere because they are recited out of habit. This type of prayer, the automatic, is seen late in *For Whom the Bell Tolls* when Maria "commenced to pray for Roberto quickly and automatically as she had done at school, saying the prayers as fast as she could and counting them on the fingers of her left hand, praying by tens of each of the two prayers she was repeating." Again, in *The Old Man and the Sea*, when Santiago becomes so fatigued that he cannot remember the words to his prayers, "he would say them fast so that they would come automatically. Hail Marys are easier to say than Our Fathers, he thought." For these characters, prayers worded as praise to spiritual figures have become reflexes by which the characters react to stress. Prayer, in becoming automatic, has lost its original meaning, but still functions for each character on a personal basis. This basis does not exclude selfish motives, getting things, and the availability as a response to stress lends another dimension to it. But the prayers themselves, recited out of habit, are insincere, and automatic prayer, therefore, is presented in as negative a light as the other types. That Hemingway has some highly sympathetic characters pray is an indication that it is prayer itself, and not the characters, that he is singling out for negative treatment.

Hemingway's treatment of prayer, which he usually depicts as selfish, ironic, desperate, or automatic, evinces a rather low regard for the practice. This negative treatment is probably due to the fact that prayer demands an acknowledgment of dependence on a superior being before whom one is powerless. Such an acknowledgment removes from the individual, at least in part, the responsibility to be self-sufficient. In making such a demand, prayer not only conflicts with a personal value of Hemingway's, but it reduces the necessity for his characters to have individual sets of values by which to live. If one relegates the practice to a minor role in which it functions for him on a personal basis, it can be integrated into an ordered, self-sufficient way of life. Anselmo's use of prayer to relieve his loneliness and Santiago's prayers to relieve the stress of his battle with the fish seem to be movements toward such integration. Even then, however, prayer tends to weaken, rather than reinforce, one's individual set of values, for, without such "ghostly comforts," one is forced to rely more on other values, ones which tap those resources that are his as a mortal man.

Prayer, then, due to the dependence implied by its very practice, is an aspect of religion that cannot serve to reinforce one's individual values. The dependence tends to replace individual values, so that the latter are not present to be reinforced. In addition, prayer fails as a primary source of benefit; selfish prayer is not a dependable method to obtain what one wants. Prayer can function for one on a personal basis but, as pointed out in the preceding paragraph, this can be detrimental to him. These seem to be the reasons why prayer is given negative treatment by Hemingway. He does depict many positive characters as praying, but their prayers rarely benefit them, more often disclosing weaknesses in their otherwise admirable characters. Lt. Berrendo, for example, is given positive treatment except at the time of his shooting Joaquin. His sign of the cross just before the act, together with his distraction by prayers for a dead comrade just afterward, make him seem foolish and humane in only a qualified way. Of primary relevance to this study, of course, is the failure of prayer as reinforcement. In this respect it is unlike membership in the clergy, which, as shown earlier, served this function well for two of Hemingway's characters.

# 3. Christian Tradition and Church Power

This chapter will concern Hemingway's treatment of two additional aspects of Christianity. One is Christian tradition, those beliefs and practices which comprise formal participation in the established Catholic and Protestant religions. The other aspect to be dealt with is the authority of the Roman Catholic Church.

In Hemingway's early works, there seems to develop a sense of skepticism toward the uses religion is put to by some people. In "The Doctor and the Doctor's Wife," for example, the doctor's wife supports her argument by sanctimoniously quoting a passage from the Bible, the traditional Christian source for religious inspiration. The passage does not serve to inspire her husband, but only increases his frustration and further alienates him from her, so that he slams the door as he stalks off. Although the Bible is made to appear absurdly irrelevant, perhaps even detrimental, to the resolution of human conflicts in this story, it is the wife's use of it that is actually given negative treatment. Being bedfast, she strives for a moral superiority over her husband to maintain dominance in the household, and she uses the Bible as an authority to affirm this righteousness. The doctor must suppress his irritation at this preaching, which opposes his first-hand practical knowledge, to avoid the guilt of upsetting the woman. She seems to be aware of this, and exploits her husband's weakness as well as the traditional teachings of the Bible. Such a use of religion, to compensate for one's personal limitations, seems, in this early story, to be an object of bitterness on Hemingway's part.

Another manifestation of this early skepticism can be seen in "The Snows of Kilimanjaro." As Harry lies in his safari camp awaiting death, one of his recollections of his past life concerns an officer with whom he had served in war. The officer was grotesquely maimed one night, and was brought in screaming for someone to shoot him. Harry further recalls that

> They had had an argument one time about Our Lord never sending you anything you could not bear and someone's theory had been that meant that at a certain time the pain passed you out automatically. But he had always remembered Williamson, that night. Nothing passed out Williamson until he gave him all his morphine tablets that he had always saved to use himself and then they did not work right away.

The skepticism expressed here seems to be directed toward man's use of religion to escape fear. The traditional idea of God not permitting unbearable pain, of His preventing its being felt, is an inadequate adjustment to the fear of such extreme suffering. A more realistic approach is more desirable, the author implies, and he has his protagonist carry morphine tablets. That the tablets are slow in working only expresses more strongly the futility of dependence on divine intervention. This supplanting of reliance on religion for more realistic responses to fear, therefore, seems to be another target of Hemingway's early skepticism.

The early skepticism expressed by Hemingway is likely the result of war experiences similar to the one described in the last example. In "Soldier's Home," which describes the isolation of a young man who has returned from similar experiences, Hemingway again describes the skepticism which has resulted from contact with warfare. When Krebs's mother tries to convince him to look for work, telling him that "God has some work for everyone to do," that "there can be no idle hands in His kingdom," Krebs replies that he is not in God's kingdom, meaning, of course, his mother's interpretation of the same. The bitterness of his statement seems to reflect that of Hemingway toward using religion to manipulate others. In citing the traditional Christian condemnation of idleness, Krebs's mother hopes to achieve a temporal objective by causing Krebs to get a job. This use of religion to control the actions of others is distasteful to Hemingway, and is therefore given negative treatment.

The effects of Hemingway's first war experiences seem to have been tempered by his later experiences, for Christian tradition appears in a more favorable light in his later works. In *Across the River and into the Trees*, for example, Col. Cantwell respectfully refers to St. Mark, and later to the Holy Grail. Attacks on the mere use of religion do not continue as strongly in these later works, but, in one respect, Hemingway still treats Christian tradition itself in a negative way. The aspects of Christianity that come under attack are those which are essentially meaningless. To clarify this statement it is necessary to distinguish between empty and meaningful forms.

Religion as Reinforcement in Hemingway

Hemingway's contempt for empty forms, which applied to other areas as well as to religion, persisted even into his later works. By empty form is meant an aspect of formal religion that has lost its original meaning but is retained on the basis of its long-standing status as a Christian tradition. In *For Whom the Bell Tolls*, for instance, Pablo orders the priests of his town to confess the Fascists he intends to execute. Since confession, in the Catholic Church, is of spiritual benefit to the penitent only when made through his own free will, its being made under duress is an empty form, a mere formality prior to execution. It was for the same reason, when Pablo had earlier ordered the members of the *guardias civiles* to kneel before he shot them, that the corporal had said, "It is as well to kneel. It is of no importance."

Another form from Christian tradition is satirized as an empty form in *Across the River and into the Trees*. Cantwell and the *Gran Maestro*, in a series of conversations, "had founded the Order of Brusadelli; noble, military and religious, and there were only five members." Although this organization might be seen chiefly as a take-off on secret societies in general, that is, groups with highly discriminating qualifications for membership, its analogy to a religious order becomes clear when Cantwell suggests a religious service in favor of their "Great Patron." The satire becomes most apparent when it is revealed that the "Great Patron," instead of possessing outstanding human qualities worthy of imitation, is simply a tax-evading millionaire who publicly blames his wife for his impotence. From this example and the one referred to above, it can be seen that, while Hemingway's treatment of Christian tradition in general grows more favorable in his later works, he does not relent toward empty forms, which he sees in religion as he does in other areas.

This comparison of Hemingway's early and later works seems to indicate that, as the artist matured, he advanced from a consistent focus on the negative applications of Christian tradition to a distinction between its meaningful aspects and its empty forms. His discrimination intensified. With regard to forms, he seems to have distinguished some which had more basic origins than their establishment as Christian traditions, that is, forms which had come into being long before they were incorporated into Christian religion. The Mass, for instance, seems to have attracted Hemingway due to its primitive origins as a sacrificial rite, rather than its incorporation into the Catholic Church. Julanne Isabelle points this out:

> Throughout history, religious rites have been recognized as capable of disciplining the mind. From the pagan incantations to Christian liturgy, people have felt the need for disciplined repetitive actions. Altar preparation became honored as a purging, cleansing, and disciplining force, making man capable of communicating with a Supreme Being. Possibly it was because of an ancient, crying need in the soul of man that Hemingway was attracted to the Mass, which represented the tradition of form and discipline that Protestant churches had modified or, in some cases, abolished. (P. 55.)

## Religion as Reinforcement in Hemingway

It is this same primitive appeal that critics such as Joseph Waldmeir have seen as the basis for Hemingway's attraction to bullfights, even drawing parallels between the two rituals. (Joseph Waldmeir, "*Confiteor Hominem*: Ernest Hemingway's Religion of Man," *Papers of the Michigan Academy of Science, Arts, and Letters*, 42 (1957), 354.) Hemingway's own understanding of the Mass's primitive origins probably helped him distinguish it from the empty forms and include it with the meaningful aspects of Christian tradition which he treated with increased respect as he matured.

A form from Christian tradition occasionally becomes meaningful for a Hemingway character because of some personal significance it holds for him. This too, however, is characteristic of the later works. In *For Whom the Bell Tolls*, Robert Jordan slays a Fascist horseman by aiming at the Sacred Heart emblem he wears on his chest. Although the established meaning of the emblem, Christ's love for mankind, does not seem relevant to the incident, Jordan's shooting at it has significance for him as an individual. Practically speaking, it is a good aiming point; symbolically, it reveals that religion, like all things, ends with death–the Sacred Heart and the heart of the Fascist are penetrated by the same bullet. In seeing this supposedly religious man shot down in an ambush, the magical qualities of the Sacred Heart emblem having failed to protect him, Jordan cannot help but be confirmed in his belief in the mortality of all things. This is reflected in his response to Maria when she expresses concern at having seen him kill a religious man. Jordan replies, "Thou saw nothing. One man. One man from a horse."

Another example of a traditional Christian form which holds personal significance for a character can be taken from *The Old Man and the Sea*. When the interior of Santiago's shack is described, it is revealed that two pictures one the wall, one of the Sacred Heart and one of the Virgin of Cobre, are relics of his wife. It is quite clear that the established meanings of these pictures are not so much present for Santiago as the secondary, personal meaning, his wife's memory. His reverence for his wife exists within forms adopted from Christian tradition, forms which reinforce his reverence by their association with virtue and holiness. These forms are treated as positive aspects of Christian tradition, and thus distinguished from those empty forms treated as negative aspects.

The mature Hemingway's increased distinction between the positive and negative aspects of Christian tradition is paralleled by his characters' focusing on specific beliefs in their attitudes toward religion. This focusing is in contrast to the general alienation toward religion manifested by the protagonists of Hemingway's early works. This transition, from the vague impressions of youth to the pondering of specific beliefs and moral questions, must be considered under Christian tradition since it is the traditional values that are eventually questioned.

The heroes of Hemingway's first two novels are examples of general dissatisfaction with religion. In the first chapter, a passage was quoted from *The Sun Also Rises* in which Jake Barnes succinctly expressed his lack of identification with Catholicism. Jake told Bill Gorton that he was "technically" a Catholic; when asked what that meant, Jake replied that he didn't know. This lack of identification with Catholicism causes Jake to attend its functions irregularly. These functions, and religion in general, never seem to attain a central position in Jake's consciousness. This is seen in Jake's description of his life in San Sebastian:

> We all had a vermouth at the café. It was a quiet life and no one was drunk. I went to church a couple of times, once with Brett. She said she wanted to hear me go to confession, but I told her that not only was it impossible but it was not as interesting as it sounded, and besides, it would be in a language she did not know. We met Cohn as we came out of church . . .

The inclusion of this reference to religious functions in the middle of a paragraph, between references to minor incidents, underscores the fact that religion is only on the periphery of Jake's consciousness, that it holds only passing interest for him. Thus, when Jake later tells Brett that he is "pretty religious," she is largely correct in answering "Oh, rot." Jake feels the need for positive values, but finds the tenets of Catholicism insufficient and is, thereby, dissatisfied with religion in a general way.

Jake's dissatisfaction is largely accounted for by the nature of the adjustment he is trying to make. As a result of a war injury, he has been left impotent; one avenue of fulfillment in life, therefore, is closed to him. The frustration he encounters can only be salved by his finding positive values that will help him adjust to his limitation. The shortcomings of Catholicism in this regard are expressed by Jake early in the novel: "The Catholic Church had an awfully good way of handling all that. Good advice, anyway. Not to think about it. Oh, it was swell advice. Try and take it sometime. Try and take it." As pointed out in the second chapter, of course, praying in the cathedral does seem to be a comforting experience for Jake; the painful thoughts of sexual problems are momentarily displaced by his rambling internal prayer. When it comes, however, to values by which Jake can make a full-scale adjustment, that is, consistently maintain his mental and emotional equilibrium despite his physical limitation, he finds the tenets of Catholicism insufficient.

Frederick Henry of *A Farewell to Arms* provides the second example. Though he admires the priest as an individual and identifies with the priest's individual values, Henry expresses a skeptical attitude toward religion as an institution:

> "I only think the Austrians will not stop when they have won a victory. It is in defeat that we become Christian."
>
> "The Austrians are Christians–except for the Bosnians."
>
> "I don't mean technically Christian. I mean like Our Lord."
>
> He said nothing.
>
> "We are all gentler now because we are beaten. How would Our Lord have been if Peter had rescued him in the Garden?"
>
> "He would have been just the same."
>
> "I don't think so," I said.

## Religion as Reinforcement in Hemingway

It should be noted that Henry's skepticism is not of values, but of religion as an institution. It is this same institution that Jake Barnes found deficient in providing the positive values he sought, values such as those seen by Henry in the priest as an individual. Like Jake, Henry feels a general dissatisfaction with religion, for he distrusts "technical" Christianity as an institution.

It is important to note that Henry's dissatisfaction is not with values, but with the formal structure and functioning of Christian religion. As was pointed out in the second chapter, and will again be discussed in the next chapter, Henry identifies, to a degree, with the values of the priest. Formal religion, however, is a failure for Henry because it fails to function on a social scale, fails to stem the avarice and brutality of a people victorious in war. In defeat, there is little choice for the victims but to be gentle and compassionate for one another's mutual benefit, but, otherwise, these positive values give way to the urge for plunder and conquest. Religion as an institution is not yet depicted as actually encouraging corruption, as it will be in *For Whom the Bell Tolls*, but it is at least seen by Henry as ineffectual in making a people more humane, and perhaps as hypocritical in pretending to do so.

The general dissatisfaction with religion expressed by these characters seems another result of Hemingway's first war experiences, which resulted in traditional Christian values losing much of their meaning for him, that is, their relevance to the solution of individual conflicts and social problems. As pointed out before, however, the effects of Hemingway's first war experiences seem to have been tempered by his later experiences. The characters of his later works, rather than expressing general dissatisfaction with religion, are concerned with specific beliefs and moral questions. Whereas Jake and Henry felt a vague lack–an uneasiness–for the reasons explained above, specific questions are raised in the later works; a few examples from the latter will clarify this.

Belief in God's existence, for example, is a recurrent motif in *For Whom the Bell Tolls*. Early in the novel, when Robert Jordan asks Anselmo if he believes in God, the old man replies, "Certainly not. If there were God, never would He have permitted what I have seen with my eyes." Anselmo cannot reconcile the existence of an all-good Supreme Being with the atrocities of war that he has witnessed; therefore, at least outwardly, he denies God's existence.

Pilar, a professed atheist like Anselmo, is less rigid in her denial. At one point she tells Jordan, "It is true that there is no sickness. There could have been. I know not why there wasn't. There probably still is God after all, although we have abolished Him." Although she's witnessed the same atrocities as Anselmo, Pilar accepts the possibility of God's existence on the basis of good fortune that she and others have experienced. This concession, which opposes her party's abolition of God, might be interpreted as stemming from superstition, rather than actual religious belief. But, more basically, it seems to grow from a need for order, which cannot be eliminated though religion might be destroyed.

Maria, who seems a simpler person than either Anselmo or Pilar, does not seem concerned with the political ideology which requires her to deny God's existence. Although she's actually been a victim of the atrocities which the others have only witnessed, her belief in God has remained unshaken. This is seen in her thoughts during the blowing of the bridge:

> She heard Pilar's big voice from away below on the hillside shouting up some obscenity to her that she could not understand and she thought, Oh, God no, no. Don't talk like that with him in peril. Don't offend anyone and make useless risks. Don't give any provocation.

She then begins to pray "quickly and automatically" for Jordan's safety, hoping to atone for Pilar's impropriety before the eyes of God. These thoughts and actions of Maria seem to indicate that her belief is grounded largely in superstition. As with Pilar, however, the more basic source of Maria's attitude toward God seems to be a need for order. Her personality and circumstances make this more apparent than with Pilar. Maria is young and alone; she has been hurt, and she needs something to make her unhappy life meaningful. Having been raised to believe in God, she clings to this belief; in moments of stress, it is her assurance against impending disaster. With God on her side, she can depend on Him to protect Jordan; without Him, she is helpless, unable to impose order on the events of the immediate future.

The question of God's existence, then, is a specific religious issue treated in Hemingway's later works. Another issue that receives extensive treatment in these works is the morality of killing. In *For Whom the Bell Tolls*, for example, Anselmo deeply regrets the killing in war, feeling that "even though necessary, it is a great sin and that afterwards we must do something very strong to atone for it." He reflects on this moral issue at great length during his watch on the mountainside. Similarly, in *The Old Man and the Sea*, Santiago ponders the morality of his killing the fish:

> You did not kill the fish only to keep alive and sell for food, he thought. You killed him for pride and because you are a fisherman. You loved him when he was alive and you loved him after. If you love him, it is not a sin to kill him. Or is it more?

Although Santiago is an admirable character and his motives for fishing free of malice, he still questions the morality of his act of killing. Similarly, Anselmo feels killing is wrong even when it is necessary. Although the killings are referred to as "sins," the moral considerations by the characters are made without reference to the tenets of their formal religion. The doctrines of Catholicism certainly deal with killing, but these traditional doctrines are insufficient to resolve the moral questions in Anselmo's and Santiago's minds.

Before Hemingway's treatment of Christian tradition can be summarized, it is first necessary to clarify the understanding of this subject that he shows in his later works. What this understanding amounts to is the realization that, although there are empty forms that have been retained in Christian religion, there are other forms, such as the Mass, with significant meaning

# Religion as Reinforcement in Hemingway

to those who participate and believe. As explained earlier, the significance of the Mass for Hemingway grew from its value as a ritual. Other forms, such as Santiago's religious pictures, became significant for individuals because of personal meanings they attached to them. Corollary to the realization that some forms are meaningful is the realization that general skepticism, such as Hemingway manifested in his early works, can be misleading; if one is too attentive to others' misuse of religion, he can be distracted from the potential value it holds for himself. With these ideas in mind, we can proceed to a more inclusive summary.

To summarize Hemingway's treatment of Christian tradition, it is again necessary to stress the greater discrimination shown by Hemingway as he matured as an artist. From his constant focus on its negative applications in his early works, Hemingway advanced to an understanding of the positive *and* negative aspects of Christian tradition. He distinguishes between its empty forms and its forms with significant meaning, and is generally more respectful toward Christian tradition than in his early works. This transition is paralleled by a change in his characters' attitudes toward religion. From the general dissatisfaction with religion shown by Jake Barnes and Frederick Henry evolves the pondering of specific beliefs and moral questions. Both of the progressions are from general to specific, and seem to be a function of Hemingway's maturity as an artist, a maturity which also entails the discovery of certain values.

For the purposes of this study, it is significant that the forms from Christian tradition found meaningful by the mature Hemingway derived their value from sources other than formal religion. Their value as rituals, or the value they acquired on a personal basis for characters, was simply reinforced by their establishment as forms from Christian tradition. In Hemingway's early works, since traditional morality did not, apparently, reinforce the knowledge gained from his own experiences, its application was given negative treatment. Christian tradition is presented as potential reinforcement in the beliefs and values of Hemingway's characters as well. Belief in God depends on one's individual personality and circumstances; one accepts the Church's stand on the morality of killing if it concurs with his personal stand. Hemingway's early protagonists were generally dissatisfied with Christian religion because it did not provide the order which they required. Its structure was inadequate to reinforce the ordered set of principles they were groping to assemble. For Jake Barnes, these principles were latent in his dedication to his work, his friendships, and his being an *aficionado*; religion, however, did not provide values that were inclusive of these latent principles, that would unify the latter into a code which, if adhered to, would provide the needed adjustment to his physical limitation. For Frederick Henry, these principles are latent in his love for Catherine, his need to escape the war, and in the values of his friends, including the priest; he cannot accept the priest's religion, however, because, although it preaches love, it fails to prevent its members from waging wars such as the one he seeks to escape. Christian tradition, then, is treated by Hemingway as a potential source of reinforcement for one's personal beliefs and values, and is seen as more valuable in this function in his later works.

As stated at the outset of this chapter, the other aspect of Christianity to be dealt with in this chapter is the authority of the Roman Catholic Church. This power is strongest, of course, over its own members, and especially relevant to Hemingway were its laws regarding marriage. These laws are a factor in "A Very Short Story." The young man and Luz, we are told, "wanted to get married, but there was not enough time for the banns, and neither of them had birth certificates." Had their marriage not been prevented by religious formalities, the ensuing tragedy would have been avoided. Catholic marriage laws, therefore, are given negative treatment in this story. They are seen as empty, outmoded forms, and as being of possible detriment to those affected by them.

Another example of the potentially bad effects of these laws is seen in *To Have and Have Not*. During an argument, Helen Gordon tells Richard that they are not really married because they were not married by a Catholic priest. "You wouldn't marry me in the Church," she says, "and it broke my poor mother's heart as well you know." The unhappiness, of course, was more basically due to the marriage laws themselves, but Helen heaps the blame onto Richard, proclaiming his inferiority to her father: "He went to Mass because my mother wanted him to and he did his Easter duty for her and for Our Lord, but mostly for her . . ." Thus, not only the marriage laws, but also other rules within the Church, are given negative treatment. Rather than being of positive value, they are depicted as sources of bitter dissension among members of a family. A case might also be made that the passage reflects Hemingway's skepticism of the use to which Helen's mother puts religion, that is, to assert her dominance in the household, a tactic employed by the wife in "The Doctor and the Doctor's Wife."

Unlike Richard Gordon, Hemingway returned to Catholicism for his marriage with Pauline Pfeiffer. However, as pointed out in the first chapter, Pauline's religion still contributed heavily to the failure of their marriage. "A good deal later," Baker relates, "he attributed the failure of his second marriage to sexual maladjustment growing out of Pauline's ardent Catholicism and the fact that she could not safely bear more children." (Baker, p. 355.) It is questionable, of course, whether Hemingway's appraisal was objective. What seems evident, however, is that he thereafter held in low esteem the Church's laws regarding marriage and sexual relations.

The power of the Church, of course, sometimes extends beyond its own members into secular matters. Hemingway was particularly concerned with this situation in Spain. The latter part of *The Sun Also Rises* is dominated by the fiesta of San Fermin, which centers around the bullfights. When one considers the drunkenness, commercialism, and thrill-seeking of which San Fermin consists, it seems ironic that it should be a religious festival. Jake senses this as he attends Mass on opening day, and a waiter expresses it more strongly after a spectator is gored. This irony, however, is only symptomatic of a more basic condition, which is expressed in *For Whom the Bell Tolls*:

> Spain has never been a Christian country. It has always had its own special idol worship within the Church. *Otra Virgen mas.* I suppose that was why they had to destroy the virgins of their enemies. Surely it was deeper with them, with Spanish religion fanatics, than it was with the people. The people had grown away from the Church because the Church was in the government and the government had always been rotten. This was the only country that the reformation never reached. They were paying for the Inquisition now, all right.

Though expressed through the consciousness of Robert Jordan, this is clearly Hemingway's own appraisal of the situation in Spain. He saw the Church's involvement in secular matters as a corrupting influence, the abandonment of spiritual values to promote the interests of a privileged class. Hemingway, therefore, had a low regard for the Church's involvement in secular matters, a position shared, of course, by many devout, non-Spanish Catholics.

Hemingway's treatment of the Church's power evinces his disapproval of religious authoritarianism. Whether within its own membership or over society in general, he saw the binding dictates of the Church as undesirable. This is in keeping with the reinforcement value he saw in religion. It was not to be obeyed against one's better judgment; its function was to reinforce the values that produced this judgment. In failing to provide reinforcement, the authority of the Church is treated even less favorably than Christian tradition, which the mature Hemingway saw as a limited source of reinforcement for personal beliefs and values.

## 4. Non-Religious Beliefs and Values

This chapter will concern those beliefs and values expressed by Hemingway and his characters which are, in fact, primary, and not secondary or reinforcing. The purpose of this discussion is to demonstrate how these primary beliefs and values are of an essentially non-religious nature. The discussion will focus first on existentialism in Hemingway's works, then on pragmatism, and then on personal values synthesized from religion and temporal interests.

The importance of existentialism to fiction can be appreciated when one considers that, according to this philosophy, man's existence precedes his essence. The latter condition is in contrast to that of all other things in the universe, each of which can only be cast into a predetermined role, an essence which is only a concept formulated prior to the thing's existence. Abraham Kaplan explains why man's difference in this regard is relevant to fiction:

> He is more than just a type, a character defined by some role or other. People of this sort are sometimes met with in fiction, and then we say in fact that the character isn't "real" but only a personified type without human personality. The author has given him a name but has failed to breathe life into him; he is only an animated

> cliché. In short, his existence is determined by an essence, but in reality the situation is exactly the reverse. The human being, in his every action, defines his own essence. (Abraham Kaplan, *The New World of Philosophy* (New York, 1961), p. 103.)

Later in this chapter, several of Hemingway's characters will be examined in light of this consideration. First, however, the writer himself should be studied, that is, the correlation determined between recurrent motifs in his works and major existential ideas. The motif most relevant in this regard, as will be explained below, is Hemingway's conception of *nada*.

In relating Hemingway's ideas to those of existentialism, it is significant that he failed to strongly identify with the teachings of formal religions. This lack of identification is similar to the position of existentialists, which is a painful awareness of the inadequacies of traditional religious philosophies. (Carl Michalson, "What Is Existentialism?" in *Christianity and the Existentialists*, ed. Carl Michalson (New York, 1956), pp. 20-22.) Traditional religion sought to define man's essence so that man might exist within a predetermined role. The existentialists, as stated above, do not believe that man's essence can predetermine his existence; they see his essence as undefined, as nothing, until he himself determines it by his existence. Hemingway's alienation from formal religion seems consistent with the interpretation that he, too, saw man's essence as originally undefined, religious explanations as based on nothingness. This is reflected in the "Our *nada*" and

James I. McGovern

"Hail nothing" thoughts in the interior monologue of the Spanish waiter in "A Clean, Well-Lighted Place."

It was probably this consciousness of man's undefined essence that inspired Hemingway in his rendering of the famous passage in *A Farewell to Arms* which concludes: "Abstract words such as glory, honor, courage, or hallow were obscene beside the concrete names of villages, the numbers of roads, the names of rivers, the numbers of regiments and the dates." The abstractions condemned in this passage, it seems, are secular attempts which seek to define man's essence, to impose upon man a predetermined role in a manner similar to that of religious philosophies. To define the essences of things, such as villages and roads, is acceptable to the existentialists; definitions of man's essence, however, are meaningless, for a man can only determine it himself by what he does.

William Barrett, in discussing this passage, sees it as "a kind of manifesto of modern art and literature, an incitement to break through empty abstractions of whatever kind . . . even if in stripping himself naked the artist seems to be left with Nothing." (William Barrett, *Irrational Man* (Garden City, N.Y., 1962), p. 45.) He goes on to say that this recognition of spiritual poverty, the encounter with nothingness, is a vital aspect of Hemingway's art and relates the latter's attitudes to his first war experiences:

> The generation of the First World War could hardly be expected to view Western culture as sacrosanct, since they perceived–and rightly– that it was bound up with the civilization that had

> ended in that ghastly butchery. Better to reject the trappings of that culture, even art itself, if that would leave one a little more honest in one's nakedness. (P. 46.)

One must encounter this nakedness, his own undefined essence, before he can determine his essence through his existence, that is, through actions which are of his own choosing. In Hemingway's works, the encounter with nothingness, or *nada*, is most strongly expressed in a short story referred to above.

In discussing "A Clean, Well-Lighted Place," Barrett compares Hemingway's story with products of the plastic arts, "those cryptic human figures in modern sculpture that are full of holes or gaps." (P. 62.) The visions presented by Hemingway and the sculptors, according to Barrett, are of a nothingness which sometimes rises up before the eyes of human beings, especially in extreme situations. In the story, one waiter seems to identify with the man at table on the basis of some shared experience, perhaps the encounter with nothingness, or *nada*. That such a basis exists, and that the identification is not of a more common sort, is stressed by Barrett later in his book:

> His words undercut the common objection that all that is involved here is a "mere mood" (as if moods were mere passiones animae, modifications inhering in a psychic substance, in the Cartesian sense). "It was not fear or dread," he tells us. "It was a nothing that he knew too well." Fear and dread are moods; but what is in question for the

character in the story is not a mood, but a presence that he knows and knows all too well. So far as the mood of Hemingway's story is concerned, it is in no way frantic, despairing, or "nihilistic." Rather, its tone is one of somber and clear courage. (Pp. 284-85.)

The reality of nothingness as a presence, then, and the probability of one's encounter with it, are of central interest in "A Clean, Well-Lighted Place." Of greater relevance to this discussion, however, is the necessity of such an awareness before one can determine his own essence. One must, after all, recognize the falseness of roles which have been imposed on him by his culture, the latter's error in attempting to define his undefinable essence, before he can, through his own free choice, choose those acts which comprise his existence and determine his essence.

The subject of existential choice can be discussed with reference to "The Short Happy Life of Francis Macomber." Through the consciousness of Wilson, the white hunter, we are made aware of the reasons for Macomber's display of bravery. Wilson, we are told,

> . . . had seen men come of age before and it always moved him. It was not a matter of their twenty-first birthday.
>
> It had taken a strange chance of hunting, a sudden precipitation into action without opportunity for worrying beforehand, to bring this about with Macomber, but regardless of how it had happened it had most certainly happened.

Although the characters speak of the change as something which has "happened," it is actually the result of Macomber's choosing to be other than a coward. His "sudden precipitation into action" is an example of the extreme situations which Barrett considers likely times for a great nothingness to rise up before the eyes of human beings. For Macomber, this nothingness included the role of coward which had previously been assigned to him; in the new crisis, the old role became meaningless. Faced with the void, with his own undefined essence, Macomber was free to choose his course of action, to define his own essence. He encountered nothingness; he chose to be brave.

Existential choice, of course, entails more than choosing courses of action; it entails what Kaplan describes as the invention of values. "Whatever meaning and value man can find in his life," he says, "must be the outcome of his own choices, his own inventions." (P. 106.) For Francis Macomber, the value chosen was to be brave. The process of inventing this value, however, does not appear to have been altogether conscious on the part of this character. For an example of clearly deliberate existential choice, that is, conscious invention of values by a character, it is necessary to refer to another of Hemingway's works.

Although changes in Robert Jordan's values occur throughout *For Whom the Bell Tolls*, it is the resolution of his final conflict which provides the clearest example of existential choice. This is because he finds himself, at this point, in his most extreme situation, feeling his most urgent need to invent values by which to make his vital decision, that is, whether or not to kill himself. His conscious invention of the crucial values is reflected in his interior monologue:

> Listen, I may have to do that because if I pass out or anything like that I am no good at all and if they bring me to they will ask me a lot of questions and do things and all and that is no good. It's much best not to have them do those things. So why wouldn't it be all right to just do it now and then the whole thing would be over with? Because oh, listen, yes, listen, *let them come now.*
>
> You're not so good at this, Jordan, he said. Not so good at this. And who is so good at this? I don't know and I don't really care just now. But you are not. That's right. You're not at all. Oh not at all, at all. I think it would be all right to do it now? Don't you?
>
> *No, it isn't.* Because there is something you can do yet. As long as you know what it is you have to do it. As long as you remember what it is you have to wait for that. *Come on. Let them come. Let them come. Let them come!*

It is noteworthy that, in making this choice, Jordan forsakes a role predetermined for him by his father's reaction in another extreme situation. Jordan invents his own values by which to make his decision, and then assumes responsibility for the consequences of his choice. For an existentialist, the supreme virtue is to be one who chooses, that is to say, to be as he has chosen. (John Wild, *The Challenge of Existentialism* (Bloomington, Ind., 1959), pp. 123-24.) Robert Jordan has attained this; he has become what existentialists call an authentic individual.

It would be hazardous, it seems, to call Hemingway an existentialist on the basis of selected examples from his works. Inconsistencies can readily be found with which to refute such a claim. One potential example is the tragedy of Harry Morgan in *To Have and Have Not*. Despite his strength and resourcefulness, his independence in making decisions, Harry can never quite achieve "authenticity" in his life. His efforts are repeatedly frustrated by his circumstances, other human beings, and the public morality. His efforts to define his own essence seem to meet insurmountable obstacles, and he concludes that "a man alone ain't got no . . . chance." According to Kaplan, however, the existentialist has an answer for such an objection to his philosophy:

> His point is that the things that merely happen to a man just don't count when he is brought up against the ultimate ground of his existence. What gives meaning to life, in the most fundamental sense, is not what happens to us but what we ourselves do. When life itself is in the balance, the things that count are not those that come from without, but those rather that are rooted in the self. (P. 123.)

A man such as Harry, of course, could hardly be expected to view things in such esoteric terms. The practical shortcomings of existentialism in a dilemma such as his remain as a potential argument against Hemingway's identification with existentialism. (One critic, however, has written a full-length work supporting

Hemingway's identification with existentialism. The critic is John Killinger and the work is *Hemingway and the Dead Gods* (Lexington, Ky., 1960.))

This mention of Hemingway viewing things in practical terms seems an appropriate cue to shift the focus of this discussion to the importance of pragmatism in Hemingway's works. The significance of this philosophy for Hemingway lay to some extent in its rejection of religious philosophy, especially its rejection of supernatural phenomena. According to John Dewey, things are to be explained, not by supernatural causation, but by their place and function in the environment. He protested that "to idealize and rationalize the universe at large is a confession of inability to master the courses of things that specifically concern us." (John Dewey, *The Influence of Darwin on Philosophy* (New York, 1910), p. 17.) The pragmatic rejection of religion, of course, is but one result of applying the *pragmatic maxim*, first formulated by Charles Peirce: "Consider what effects, that might conceivably have practical bearings, we conceive the object of our conception to have. Then our conception of these effects is the whole of our conception of the object." (Charles Peirce, *The Collected Papers of Charles Sanders Peirce*, ed. Charles Hartshorne and Paul Weiss (Cambridge, Mass., 1931-35), V, 402.) The belief in transcendent beings or processes, and abstract values in general, are thus rejected by the pragmatist. The meaning of an idea is determined by the practical consequences of its application to one's life or to society; values must have their basis in experience. The relevance of such a philosophy to Hemingway is

## Religion as Reinforcement in Hemingway

best illustrated by direct reference to his works.

The fifteenth vignette of *In Our Time* provides an illustration of Hemingway's pragmatic evaluation of abstract values. The two priests at Sam Cardinella's hanging advise him to "be a man" and also hold a crucifix before his face. Such abstract values are irrelevant to Sam in his situation, however; he responds only to the cap he must wear during his execution. To speak in terms of the pragmatic maxim, the idea of being a man and the idea embodied by the crucifix are simply of no bearing on the conduct of Sam Cardinella's life; the values offered by the priests are false. This is emphasized in the closing sentence of the vignette: "The priest skipped back onto the scaffolding just before the drop fell." Being a man and revering the crucifix were no substitutes for the safety of the scaffolding.

An example of more practical values may be drawn from *Green Hills of Africa*. Near the end of this work, Hemingway feels guilty when he wounds a sable bull but allows him to escape, for the bull is then easy prey for hyenas. This illustrates a tenet of the morality of hunters, an idea of meaning because its application has definite practical consequences for the creatures in one's environment. Hemingway feels his deed was wrong not because it violates some abstract moral code, but because his experience shows it to be so. He knows that, as a result of his act, the bull will suffer; he has failed the animal, not a transcendent being.

The example just cited can be used to illustrate the principle of contextualism, by which the pragmatist puts every problem into its concrete behavioral and social setting, analyzing every idea as an abstraction from some context of action. Hemingway analyzed his experience with the bull in light of the ecological matrix in which it occurred. In another context, namely, if he hadn't wounded the bull to start, he would not have felt guilty for not killing it. Each problem must be solved individually as it occurs; Kaplan explains why:

> Contextualism means that no problem can be solved once for all, for the simple reason that we can confront a problem only in the situation in which we happen to find ourselves; in other situations, the problems that we will face will also be quite other. There are no ultimates, no absolutes, because there is no ultimate and absolute context ... (P. 20.)

Related to this disavowal of ultimates and absolutes is the evolutionary approach taken by pragmatists. By keeping in mind the constant growth or change exhibited by all things, the pragmatist sees the attainment of some perfect state as an illusion. John Dewey outlines the alternative:

> Not perfection as a final goal, but the ever-enduring process of perfecting, maturing, refining, is the aim of living ... The bad man is the man who, no matter how good he has been, is beginning to deteriorate, to grow less good. The good man is the man who, no matter how morally unworthy he *has* been, is moving to become better. Such a conception makes one severe in judging himself

and humane in judging others. (John Dewey, *Reconstruction in Philosophy* (New York, 1920), pp. 176-77.)

Dewey's moral criteria can be applied to Pablo of *For Whom the Bell Tolls*. In the eyes of Pilar, he has "gone bad" because he is no longer willing to expend himself for the success of the revolution; the judgment is made in spite of Pablo's past achievements. Pilar, of course, is a communist, and her cause largely ideological. A pragmatist with broader vision might see Pablo's change as being for the better, judging him as a good man despite his past participation in the atrocities of war. In either case, it is the direction of change that is judged, not the cumulative effects of the man's actions.

Contextualism and the evolutionary approach, it seems, imply that religious doctrine is irrelevant for the pragmatist in making moral judgments. If there are no ultimate or absolute truths, then it is erroneous to conform to permanent moral principles formulated by a formal religion or other social institution. If a man is good or bad on the basis of his direction of growth, then it is misleading to sanctify or condemn him on the basis of his good or bad works. Although these ideas are reflected to some extent in Hemingway's works, it would be hazardous to label him a pragmatist. There are, after all, serious flaws in this philosophy, flaws which Hemingway brings to light in one of his less heralded works.

In *To Have and Have Not*, Harry Morgan's values have their basis in his experience; His morality is dictated by what he feels he must do to support his family. In this way he is a pragmatist and, at the outset of the book, seems to be doing well. But, with the onset of the Depression, he finds his fishing clientele drastically reduced, and so must offer his boat and navigating skill to smugglers. He remains pragmatic, suffering no moral conflicts, even after his murder of Mr. Sing. His philosophy, that is, his way of life, functions for him as an individual; in the eyes of society, however, it is dysfunctional, for the practical consequences of its application include disruption of the social order, violation of the laws. Society, then, judges Harry's actions immoral, and it should be noted that the judgment is based on pragmatic considerations. Harry's morality conflicts with that of society, even though both are pragmatic, and this leads to Harry's downfall. This, it seems, illustrates a basic weakness of pragmatism: it leaves too little room for individualism. It is a philosophy most useful as a social control, of value primarily to those with vested interests in a particular social structure.

As stated at the outset, the final item to be discussed in this chapter is Hemingway's presentation of personal values synthesized from religion and temporal interests. One way in which this synthesis works can be seen in the comments of several characters from Hemingway's early works. In *The Sun Also Rises*, Brett muses, "You know it makes one feel rather good deciding not to be a bitch," that "It's sort of what we have instead of God." She sees her own temporal value from a religious perspective; the personal value itself is in no way religious. A second example is seen in *A Farewell to Arms* when Catherine tells Henry that she has no religion, but then adds, "You're my religion. You're all I've got." Here again, the character sees her own temporal value from a religious perspective. A final example in which this occurs, and in which the personal value itself is in no way religious, can be drawn from "The Light of the World." In the latter story, a boxer is glorified by a prostitute, who says, "I loved him like you love God," that "He was like a god, he was. So white and clean and beautiful and smooth and fast and like a tiger or like lightning."

A more complex and significant synthesis of personal values from religion and temporal interests occurs in *A Farewell to Arms*. This synthesis consists of the resolution of what may be termed the priest-Henry-Rinaldi triangle. Of the three points of view expressed by these characters, the priest's and Rinaldi's are clearly defined but Henry's is more ambiguous. What Henry actually seems to do, as the novel progresses, is synthesize personal values from aspects of each of the two other points of view. While Henry shows no inclination to adopt the priest's religion, he is attracted to the clear, cold, dry country of the priest's homeland and the spiritual uplifting which it symbolizes. Rinaldi, as a surgeon, is concerned with the body rather than the spirit; his personal interests are temporal and sensual. Though Henry is repelled by the scene of bloodshed in which Rinaldi functions best professionally, he shares the surgeon's interests in sensual gratification and strong comradeship.

It is tempting to conclude that Henry completes his synthesis by fleeing to the mountains with Catherine, for there he can experience the spiritual uplifting of clear, cold, dry country while sharing sensual gratification with

Catherine. It doesn't seem to be that simple, however. With the appearance of Count Greffi before Henry's departure, there is an indication that the resolution of the triangle has yet to be completed. Although he knows what he wants, and temporarily obtains it, Henry's awareness has not yet been tempered by the experience manifested by the old count. It is with Catherine's death that his synthesis of the priest's and Rinaldi's values is completed, for he then realizes the limits within which his personal values can be applied, limits marked by the deaths of all things.

For an example of personal values synthesized from religion and temporal interests in Hemingway's later works, it seems advisable to look to *Across the River and into the Trees*. After an early discussion of the madonnas of the Italian painters, Cantwell obtains a portrait of Renata which he treats as a religious image, talking to it in Renata's absence as one might pray to the Blessed Virgin or a saint. He carries Renata's jewels like a rosary, and later desires to give her a garment of duck plumage, "the way the old Mexicans used to ornament their gods." Cantwell's admiration for Renata is expressed in religious ways, but with no pretense to the actual beliefs from which they derive. In using religious forms to express his feelings, he is seeing his own temporal values from a religious perspective, resulting in his veneration of the young woman he loves.

Hemingway's treatment of non-religious beliefs and values differs in an essential way from his treatment of aspects of religion, which was discussed in previous chapters. Whether the values are discussed in terms of existentialism, pragmatism, or beliefs synthesized

## Religion as Reinforcement in Hemingway

from religion and temporal interests, they are primary, not reinforcing. The values discussed in this chapter originate within the individual, while the religious values were assimilated by the individual from without to order or bolster his confidence in his personal, primary values. For Hemingway, it seems, one's most basic beliefs and values must be formed within himself as an individual man; standardized values, such as those drawn from religion, can serve only secondary, reinforcing purposes.

# 5. Believing in Belief

In this, the concluding chapter, an attempt will be made to summarize the arguments and evidence presented in the previous chapters in order to draw all of the threads together into a cohesive restatement. By this means, it is hoped, the truth and significance of the consideration here being made can more easily be evaluated.

The thesis of this study was that Hemingway treated religion as a thing of secondary importance, a social phenomenon of value to the extent that it reinforces beliefs that one already holds. Due consideration was also given to its possible function on personal bases for individual characters, and the consequent reinforcement of Hemingway's own beliefs. The initial chapter consisted of relevant biographical material, with correlations noted between the man's experience and incidents in his works. Events of primary importance to the thesis included Hemingway's early alienation from Protestantism, his parents' influence in this regard, his experience in World War I and conversion to Catholicism, his later reconversion to marry Pauline Pfeiffer, and his disenchantment with the Church for its support of the Fascists in Spain.

The three periods during which Hemingway practiced a formal religion, his three departures from such practice, as well as his mature attitude of neither acceptance nor rejection, seem to indicate not only a belief in the possibility of religion's functioning in some way for an individual, but also growing disillusion concerning the possibility of its functioning in certain ways for Hemingway himself. What these ways were must be derived from the man's writings, his artistic expressions of the ideas that were foremost in his mind. His treatment of several aspects of Christianity, discussed in the second and third chapters, reflects his ideas on the potential value of religion as reinforcement for himself and other individuals.

In discussing Hemingway's treatment of the clergy, it was pointed out that, for Sister Cecilia and the priest of *A Farewell to Arms*, formal religion served to order those definite values by which they lived. It was due to their personal traits and values that Hemingway treated them in a positive way, not the religion which encouraged those traits and ordered those values. In providing this order, religion functions as reinforcement for these members of the clergy. Yet Hemingway's protagonists, even though they admire these religious for their ordered sets of values and, in Henry's case, identify with the values themselves, never seriously consider becoming Catholic. These cases, quite clearly, are expressions of a belief in religion being of potential value to an individual as reinforcement, but also of an awareness that it cannot function in this way for everyone. Hemingway's own futile attempts to practice Catholicism lend credence to this deduction; its tenets were too incongruent to adequately function as reinforcement for his personal values. The natures of these incongruencies are discovered in his treatment of the other aspects of Christianity.

In the discussion of prayer, it was concluded that Hemingway's negative treatment of the practice is due to its demand for an acknowledgment of dependence on a superior being, an acknowledgment which reduces the necessity for his characters to have individual sets of values by which to live. That such dependence should replace individual responsibility, of course, was unacceptable to Hemingway, and this dependence also made prayer valueless as reinforcement; the dependence tends to replace individual values so that the latter are not present to be reinforced. Although prayer occasionally seemed to function for a character on a personal basis, such as Anselmo's praying to relieve his loneliness, it was still seen as detrimental, for it weakened the character's tendency to rely on his own human abilities to solve his problems. Hemingway, it seems, saw little or no real value in prayer, for, not only was its practice incongruent with his conception of himself, but it seemed worthless or detrimental in the construction of any individual set of values.

The discussion of Christian tradition stressed Hemingway's progression from a sense of skepticism toward certain uses of religion to an ability to distinguish its meaningful aspects, such as the Mass, from its empty forms. Parallel to this progression was a change in his characters' attitudes; whereas the early protagonists manifested general dissatisfaction with religion, later characters pondered specific beliefs and moral questions. The Mass was one aspect of Christian tradition that was of value to Hemingway himself; others, such as Santiago's religious pictures, had meanings for

## Religion as Reinforcement in Hemingway

individual characters that they did not necessarily have for the writer. It was noted, however, that the meaning Hemingway saw in the Mass arose from its value as a ritual, so that its religious context was secondary to the writer, or, in terms of the thesis, reinforcing. Similarly, the religious contexts were secondary to the personal meanings that certain Christian forms held for Hemingway's characters. With the change in his characters' attitudes toward religion, Christian tradition again emerged as potential reinforcement; as shown in the third chapter, one's belief in God depended on one's individual personality and circumstances, and one accepted the Church's stand on the morality of killing if it concurred with one's personal stand.

As were pointed out, there are frequent instances of empty forms and conflicts between personal and traditional Christian values even in Hemingway's later works. Thus, although Christian tradition is seen as being of some value as reinforcement, it is also seen as somewhat limited in serving this function. For Hemingway himself, it seems, there were too few reinforcing aspects of Christian tradition for him to permanently embrace a formal religion. Seen from this viewpoint, his three departures from the practice of formal religion are more understandable.

Regarding the authority of the Roman Catholic Church, it was concluded that Hemingway saw its binding dictates as undesirable, whether directed at its own members or at society in general, as in Spain. This view, it was pointed out, is in keeping with the reinforcement value he saw in religion. It was not to be obeyed against one's better judgment; its function was to reinforce the values that produced this judgment. The negative effects of the Church's power on individuals and society, as well as its lack of positive value as reinforcement, were probably factors in Hemingway's inability to permanently embrace Catholicism. Together with his feelings toward prayer and the non-reinforcing aspects of Christian tradition, these factors seem to account, to a great extent, for the writer's disinclination toward the practice of a formal religion.

The fourth chapter dealt with primary, as opposed to reinforcing, values in Hemingway's works, with the purpose of demonstrating that they were of an essentially non-religious nature. Primary values expressed by the writer and his characters were shown to correlate with ideas drawn from existentialism and pragmatism, two philosophies that are generally formulated apart from religious considerations. Other primary values were shown to be synthesized from religion and temporal interests; religion, as one element of these compounds, seemed to serve a personal function, apart from reinforcement, for the characters involved. Whether through existential choice, through applying the pragmatic maxim, or through deliberate or subconscious synthesis, the values discussed in this chapter originated within the individual. They contrast with the religious values, discussed earlier, which were assimilated by the individual from without to reinforce his personal, primary, values. Though the synthesized values can only be safely attributed to his characters, the existential and pragmatic values were probably, to some extent, Hemingway's own. With this in mind, it is not difficult to understand his failure to find reinforcement of his personal values in the practice of formal religion.

The foregoing summary, it seems, is a sufficient restatement of the points expounded in the earlier chapters; it also suggests one or two minor qualifications of the original thesis. First, it seems necessary to stress that religion is not of equal value as reinforcement for every individual. This is seen in the varying ways and degrees to which religion served this function for Hemingway's characters. Only in a few instances did it serve this function so well for a character that he was really devoted to the practice of formal religion. For Hemingway himself, it seems, religion was disappointing in serving this function. Perhaps a second qualification to be made in accepting the thesis would take note of the ways discovered in which religion functions on personal bases for characters apart from reinforcement. This was seen chiefly in the discussions of prayer and of personal values synthesized from religion and temporal interests. It is noteworthy that, in depicting these functions other than reinforcement, Hemingway was enabled to express his themes, so that his ideas were reinforced in the eyes of the reader; thus, religion still functioned, albeit indirectly, as reinforcement.

That a man should value religion as reinforcement of his personal values should not, it seems, be interpreted as opposition to those who practice religion in expectation of a life hereafter. Rather, it is a stance taken by a man oriented toward the concrete, toward people he can relate with frankly, pleasures and pains he can sense strongly, and in this life. To get the most out of this life, and to get it fairly, Hemingway saw the necessity that this life be ordered, and the potential value of religion in contributing to this order. He took his stance not as a philosopher opposing the adherents to another philosophy, but, as he tried to do all things, as an individual man.

# Bibliography

Baker, Carlos. *Ernest Hemingway: A Life Story.* New York: Scribner's, 1969.

_____. "The Mountain and the Plain." *The Virginia Quarterly Review*, 27 (1951), 410-18.

Barrett, William. *Irrational Man: A Study in Existential Philosophy.* Garden City, N.Y.: Doubleday Anchor Books, 1962.

Beever, Anthony. *The Spanish Civil War.* New York: Peter Bedrick Books, 1983.

Dewey, John. *The Influence of Darwin on Philosophy.* New York: H. Holt and Company, 1910.

_____. *Reconstruction in Philosophy.* New York: H. Holt and Company, 1920.

Donaldson, Scott. *By Force of Will: The Life and Art of Ernest Hemingway.* New York: New York Press, 1977.

Flora, Joseph M. *Hemingway's Nick Adams.* Baton Rouge: Louisiana State University Press, 1982.

Fuentes, Norberto. *Hemingway in Cuba.* Secaucus, N.J.: Lyle Stuart, 1984.

Hemingway, Ernest. *In Our Time.* New York: Scribner's, 1925.

_____. *The Sun Also Rises.* New York: Scribner's, 1926.

_____. *The Snows of Kilimanjaro and Other Stories.* New York: Scribner's, 1927.

_____. *A Farewell to Arms.* New York:

Scribner's, 1929.

———. *Death in the Afternoon.* New York: Scribner's, 1932.

———. *Winner Take Nothing.* New York: Scribner's, 1933.

———. *Green Hills of Africa.* New York: Scribner's, 1935.

———. *To Have and Have Not.* New York: Scribner's, 1937.

———. *For Whom the Bell Tolls.* New York: Scribner's, 1940.

———. *Across the River and into the Trees.* New York: Scribner's, 1950.

———. *The Old Man and the Sea.* New York: Scribner's, 1952.

Hertzel, Leo J. "Hemingway and the Problem of Belief." *Catholic World*, Oct. 1956, pp. 29-33.

Hicks, Granville. "Love and Death and Hemingway." Review of *Hemingway and the Dead Gods*, by John Killinger. *Saturday Review*, 14 Jan. 1961, p. 15.

Howe, Irving. "In Search of a Moral Style." *The New Republic*, 25 Sept. 1961, pp. 21-23.

Isabelle, Julanne. *Hemingway's Religious Experience.* New York: Vantage Press, 1964.

Kaplan, Abraham. *The New World of Philosophy.* New York: Vintage Books, 1961.

Kert, Bernice. *The Hemingway Women.* New York: W. W. Norton, 1983.

Killinger, John. *Hemingway and the Dead Gods: A Study in Existentialism.* Lexington, Ky.: University of Kentucky Press, 1960.

Michalson, Carl. "What Is Existentialism?" In

*Christianity and the Existentialists*, edited by Carl Michalson. New York: Charles Scribner's Sons, 1956.

Nagel, James, editor. *Ernest Hemingway: The Writer in Context.* Madison: University of Wisconsin Press, 1984.

Peirce, Charles S. *The Collected Papers of Charles Sanders Peirce*, edited by Charles Hartshorne and Paul Weiss. Cambridge, Mass.: Harvard University Press, 1935.

Reynolds, Michael S. *Hemingway's First War.* Princeton, N.J.: Princeton University Press, 1976.

Stanton, Edward F. *Hemingway and Spain.* Seattle: University of Washington Press, 1989.

Waldmeir, Joseph. "*Confiteor Hominem*: Ernest Hemingway's Religion of Man." *Papers of the Michigan Academy of Science, Arts, and Letters*, 42 (1957), 349-56.

Wild, John. *The Challenge of Existentialism.* Bloomington, Ind.: Indiana University Press, 1959.

# About the Author

James I. McGovern holds a graduate degree in literature and has taught at the college level. He has written numerous articles, stories, and books. Mr. McGovern currently resides in northern Illinois.